The Acquirer's Playbook: A Little Process Map That Works
Copyright © 2015 Ian D Smith

Booking for speaking, corporate training and media appearances available through The Portfolio Partnership.

Call 978 395 1155

Portfoliopartnership.com

Cover & book design by Nu-Image Design

Edited by Christopher Keith
cwkeith112@gmail.com.

Published in the United States by CreateSpace, an Amazon company

ISBN-13: 978-1512197556

THE
ACQUIRER'S
PLAYBOOK

A LITTLE PROCESS MAP THAT WORKS

Author – Ian D. Smith, B.A.,C.A.

Ian founded The Portfolio Partnership (TPP) in 2009. TPP is an operational consultancy focused on scaling private businesses organically and by acquisition. Ian's experience building four previous businesses in publishing, investment banking, and software in both Europe and the United States gives him a unique set of skills and a sense of humor. As an ex-CFO, investment banker, venture capitalist, and CEO, Ian has realized more than $400 million for shareholders over the past 25 years

Ian has been creating remarkable businesses since the early 80s with Thomson (now Thomson Reuters), creating Livingstone Guarantee, an early leading investment banking boutique, as the second employee, building the FTSE 100 Capita Group

in the 1990s, and turning around software businesses in Boston over the last decade. Since 2009, Ian has been working alongside owners and leaders to build remarkable businesses. These are intensive relationships working on the operational playbooks that change the trajectory of companies. Several of the Partnership's private clients are consistently ranked in the Inc. 5000 honors list.

TPP delivers interim CEO, COO and CFO executives as part of your C-level team deploying our unique, successful playbooks to scale your business. TPP offers a dedicated acquisition support team for those clients seeking growth through acquisition.

Ian's hobbies include writing and running. He has published seven books and around 500 blog posts. Ian's last book, *Fulfilling the Potential of Your Business*, won a Small Biz Book Award for Management. He competes on the track for Mass Velocity and in 2015 is ranked #4 in the world at 400m indoors in his M55 age class. Ian graduated from the University of Strathclyde and is a member of the Institute of Chartered Accountants of Scotland. Ian holds both US and UK citizenship.

Reach out to me at
ian.smith@portfoliopartnership.com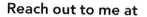
to discuss your Acquisition issues or call 978 395 1155

Contents – The Acquirer's Playbook

Introduction

Acquisitions can quantum leap growth. Acquisitions allow a transformation of scale. They can accelerate the execution of a great strategy, but they require a process to ensure success.

Almost all research done points to around 50% of acquisitions being a failure in the eyes of the acquirer. Research conducted by Cass Business School concludes that price is not the determining factor for success but that post-acquisition integration is the key.

In fact, specific research on experienced acquirers reveals that only those that invest in post-mortems after the deal get better at doing deals (Heimeriks, Gates and Zollo). We all know, it's not so much how much we do of something, it's how we much learn each time we do it.

Remember—acquisition is not a strategy. Acquisition is a tactical technique to achieve a well thought through strategy. First, define your unique market. Then use various techniques to dominate.

Buy what you want to buy, not what is up for sale. The most expensive acquisition you may ever make is the $1 price tag purchased out of Chapter 11 because the post-acquisition costs to fix it run into the millions of dollars.

Be prepared to train yourself to become an acquirer. Buy in or recruit key people to execute acquisitions alongside your team.

So why do them? Why take the risk of acquisitions? Because scale matters. Building a business to define and dominate a unique market is the secret to beating the odds against creating something of value. Acquisitions can quantum leap growth. You can be remarkable or invisible. Your choice.

The benefits of acquisitions:

- An acquirer knows that doing a small deal is as painful as doing a large deal, so given a choice, an acquirer will plump for the bigger private company. Therefore size has a big impact on your ability to be acquired.

- In the same sector with similar growth prospects, the larger company will attract a higher multiple of profits from an acquirer in pricing the deal.

- The higher the market share, the higher the profit margins and the better the trade terms from vendors.

- The acquisition of special people can sometimes only be achieved by an acquisition. So you could argue the acquisition of Groove by Microsoft was actually the acquisition of Ray Ozzie.

- Now, keeping great people post-acquisition takes careful planning and the creation of an entrepreneurial culture. Google's acquisition of Applied Semantics helped them develop the text-advertising network called AdSense that is now a multibillion-dollar revenue generator.

- Acquisitions can allow you to offer your key customers solutions you know they need, especially as your industry is transforming. E.g., advertising agencies need to offer their clients real digital talent including development expertise.

- Scale brings the ability to spread bigger marketing budgets, R&D, sales costs over more customers.

- A smart acquisition can bring a new attractive business model into the family that can be nurtured over time.

- All businesses are in the talent war, both acquiring it and nurturing it. Acquisitions bring a new level of growth prospects to a company, and staff are always attracted to an exciting narrative.

- Speed of movement. A well-executed acquisition integrated successfully can shave years off the timetable of your strategic plans.

The Acquirer's Playbook is the narrative detailing how to execute a better process map, a better playbook. That process map is called The Acquisition Approvals Model. It is a detailed process map in six simple phases with 25 sequential stages which you can embed in your business. It takes a complex transaction and simplifies it into actions you can execute.

The Acquisition Approvals Model itself, of course, needs to be translated into each specific industry, adapted to the economics, the culture, the vocabulary of each vertical market.

Carefully calibrate the Acquisition Approvals Model to your own circumstances.

This little book will change the way you buy companies. It will force your post-acquisition integration plan to the top of the agenda. It will significantly change the odds of successfully completing the right deals at the right price and integrating them seamlessly.

Turn the page and examine the Acquisition Approvals Model. This book will walk you through each stage with practical advice on how to successfully execute and integrate targets.

All businesses are in the talent war, both acquiring it and nurturing it. Acquisitions bring a new level of growth prospects to a company, and staff are always attracted to an exciting narrative.

THE ACQUISITION APPROVALS MODEL

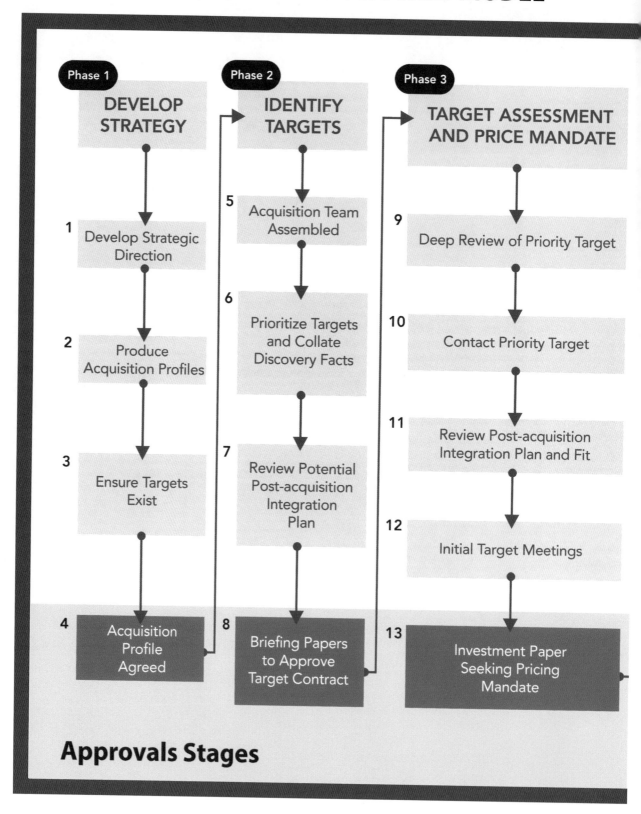

Phase 1

DEVELOP STRATEGY

1. Develop Strategic Direction
2. Produce Acquisition Profiles
3. Ensure Targets Exist
4. Acquisition Profile Agreed

Phase 2

IDENTIFY TARGETS

5. Acquisition Team Assembled
6. Prioritize Targets and Collate Discovery Facts
7. Review Potential Post-acquisition Integration Plan
8. Briefing Papers to Approve Target Contract

Phase 3

TARGET ASSESSMENT AND PRICE MANDATE

9. Deep Review of Priority Target
10. Contact Priority Target
11. Review Post-acquisition Integration Plan and Fit
12. Initial Target Meetings
13. Investment Paper Seeking Pricing Mandate

Approvals Stages

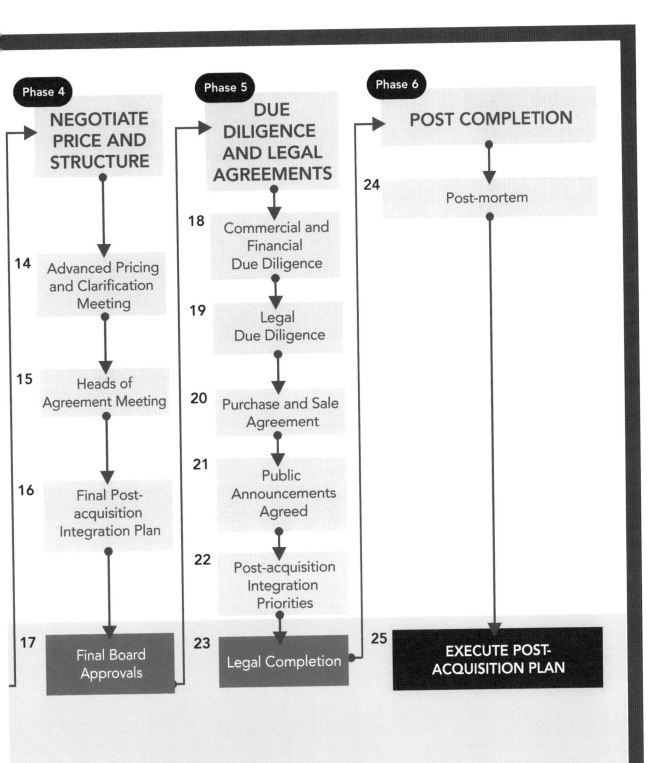

Phase 4

NEGOTIATE PRICE AND STRUCTURE

14 Advanced Pricing and Clarification Meeting

15 Heads of Agreement Meeting

16 Final Post-acquisition Integration Plan

17 Final Board Approvals

Phase 5

DUE DILIGENCE AND LEGAL AGREEMENTS

18 Commercial and Financial Due Diligence

19 Legal Due Diligence

20 Purchase and Sale Agreement

21 Public Announcements Agreed

22 Post-acquisition Integration Priorities

23 Legal Completion

Phase 6

POST COMPLETION

24 Post-mortem

25 EXECUTE POST-ACQUISITION PLAN

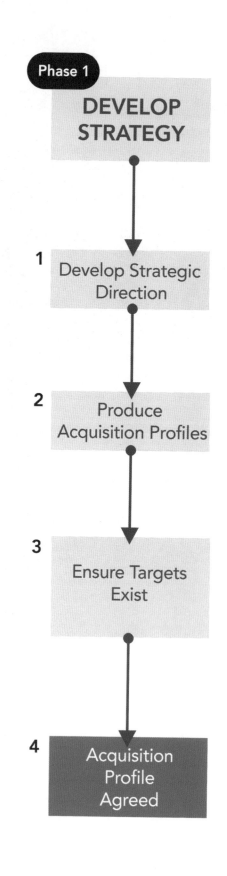

Phase 1

DEVELOP STRATEGY

1 Develop Strategic Direction

2 Produce Acquisition Profiles

3 Ensure Targets Exist

4 Acquisition Profile Agreed

Phase 1 – Develop Strategy

This first phase of the Acquisition Approvals Model is focused on defining who you are. What is your strategy? Remember strategy is what you leave out. Acquisitions are a terrible idea if you're unclear in which direction you want to travel.

STAGE 1 – DEVELOP STRATEGIC DIRECTION

I can't stress enough the importance of understanding who you are, what your core competencies are, because getting that wrong can be fatal. You need to be damn sure you can integrate the target and that you can run it better than the seller. Remember you are not just buying the house; you are buying the family inside it! You want to buy what you want to buy, not what is up for sale. Acquisitions are just a tool to enable the execution of your strategy. They are not a strategy on their own.

If you are embarking on an acquisition strategy for the first time and reviewing the best direction to take the business, then I'd recommend conducting a Strategic Workshop.

The away day, the retreat, the jamboree. They have all been discredited by abuse. But there is a really powerful, one to two-day event that I would recommend to a management team in the process of validating their acquisition strategy – The Strategic Workshop.

These are the key ingredients to a successful outcome:

Remind your senior management team why reviewing your strategy is crucial to success. Explain to them the importance of "Zooming Out" as well as "Zooming In" (Collins and Hansen). Remind them of recent examples of large successful companies missing the bend in the road, e.g., Motorola, Nokia, Blackberry, Kodak, Oracle. Big companies get complacent, lazy, overconfident. They miss things. Taking time out to review strategy could be the key to your success.

Remind them this is a great technique for reviewing the best way forward. To really rehearse potential market segments that you could dominate based on your unique skills. This is no easy task. There is still too much mystery interpreting the significance of market events, e.g., Banking, HR, Healthcare, Media, Music, Software, and Automotive sectors have all been generating a plethora of signals to their respective players that repositioning is essential!

Invite each participant to the workshop to produce an essential position paper to distribute in advance of the workshop. This builds great engagement to the debate

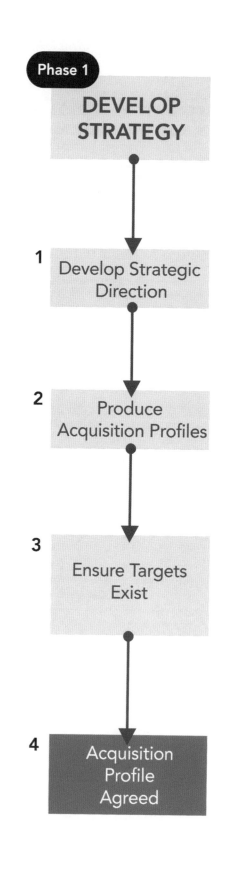

and ensures issues are thoroughly researched. To allow thoughts in the workshop to flow smoothly, limit the agenda items to a maximum of three. But they must be three big key issues that will help drive the business forward.

Appoint an external moderator.

Hold the workshop offsite, and ban the use of cell phones during each session. Allocate the time efficiently to ensure the three agenda items are covered. All agenda items must end in clear next steps (which could be as simple as detailed research to establish the key facts). The minimum outcome for each agenda item should be a set of questions you need to answer, at some point, in the next 4 weeks.

You have to be careful that these workshops don't become witch-hunts. It's too easy for powerful managers to gang up on one weak manager. Control personal attacks by focusing on the business agenda. Typical outcomes to Strategic Workshops focused on Acquisitions include:

I can't stress enough the importance of understanding who you are, what your core competencies are, because getting that wrong can be fatal.

- Restructuring of organization charts.
- Launching of a new acquisition direction focused on specific targets.
- Launching of new products.
- Aborting a losing idea.
- Total overhaul of the marketing content strategy.
- Revamping of the company's business model.
- A much tighter definition of what business the company is in!

Aligning your acquisition strategy perfectly with your company's mission has tremendous benefits:

- Your story becomes more compelling to your own employees.
- Head Office (where relevant) buy-in to the strategic direction you have chosen. This will be important later when targets are presented to the Board for sign-off.
- When you meet targets for the first time, you need to have a compelling story of why you want to buy them. Don't underestimate the importance to an owner of non-price issues like what happens to their employees.
- Being clear on who you are and what you want to become is critical to setting a post-acquisition integration plan for each target. The integration plan will have authenticity. It will sound like you've thought it through because you have.

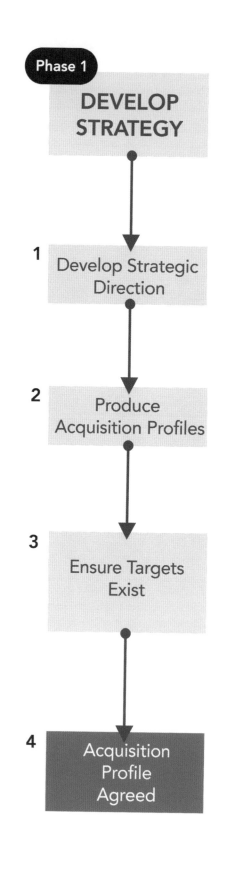

Phase 1

DEVELOP STRATEGY

1 Develop Strategic Direction

2 Produce Acquisition Profiles

3 Ensure Targets Exist

4 Acquisition Profile Agreed

STAGE 2 – PRODUCE ACQUISITION PROFILES

Because you are clear on your strategic direction, it is possible to create a shopping list. This is not a list of names but rather a list of key characteristics of the type of targets that fit your strategy. This document is your Acquisition Profile.

The Profile can be used both internally and externally to inform trusted advisers and relevant connections in your network to increase deal volume being brought to you.

Here is an illustrative example from the software world:

ACQUISITION PROFILE

Investment Thesis: Purchase a software company that has the potential to dominate a unique niche and grow the company into a $100+ million market segment leader.

Key Elements of Strategy:
1. Recurring revenue model providing a "utility-like" capability to end-users
2. Compelling and easily communicated value proposition to end users with the potential to be disruptive to legacy business practices
3. Defensible, niche application within a space that we can define and dominate
4. End-user market that is $500 million to $1 billion so as to be attractive to us but does not attract the large software competitors
5. Strong underlying code with improvement opportunities in the business processes of the company
6. Under-achieving relative to the market potential of the software's capabilities
7. Purchased at a reasonable price relative to current performance and growth opportunities to take advantage of the current market environment

Target Characteristics:
1. Model: SaaS or hybrid SaaS/on-premise software model
2. Revenues: $10 – 30 million
3. Geography
   - Tier I – Eastern MA, Southern NH and Southern MA
   - Tier II – New England
   - Tier III – Northeast U.S.
   - Tier IV – West Coast
4. History: preferably 10 years of operation
5. Legal Status: Private or Subsidiary/Division of Public Company
6. Assessment of Qualified Candidates:
   - Revenue growth & Profit Margin
   - Age of company
   - Industry vertical
   - Functional activity served
   - Operational fitness

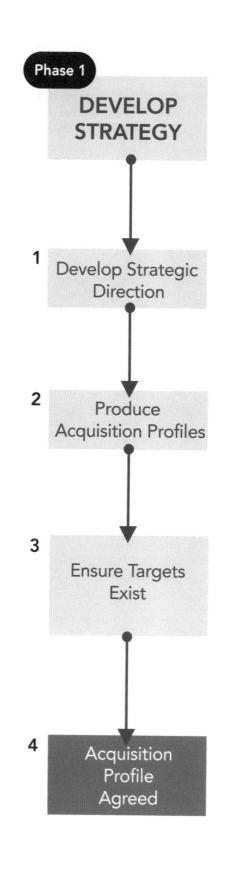

Phase 1

DEVELOP STRATEGY

1 Develop Strategic Direction

2 Produce Acquisition Profiles

3 Ensure Targets Exist

4 Acquisition Profile Agreed

Acquisition profiles are living documents. They need to be reviewed regularly for relevance. Often because an acquisition strategy involves confidential diversification into contiguous sectors, these profiles can only be shared with a discrete, well-qualified audience. Nevertheless, by articulating the type of businesses that make sense, acquirers are forced to focus on businesses they should be buying, not what is up for sale.

I've seen acquisition profiles include companies in distress. The profile states that loss-making targets should be considered. I would urge caution in attempting turnarounds unless you have built up a track record of success. Perhaps you've done some small deals that were loss makers and had great success. However, the most expensive acquisitions are ones that are acquired for a $1 but the post-acquisition costs to fix them are crushing.

Even huge companies that have done many acquisitions can underestimate the cost of fixing a problem. The acquisition of Countrywide by Bank of America for $2.5 billion, according to some estimates, has run up a post-acquisition cost of an additional $47.5 billion!

So think carefully on what you want to buy. Consider the skillsets of your team and consider at this early stage how these types of target companies will be run under your ownership.

STAGE 3 – ENSURE TARGETS EXIST

It is important to check that targets exist that match your precise Acquisition Profile. E.g., one initial Acquisition Profile described securing a software company with sales in excess of $50m in a geographical region with specific features. It produced zero targets. Think again. Another Acquisition Profile defined targets too broadly regarding a generic set of characteristics for US distribution companies. The profile produced 1000s of candidates – refinement clearly was needed.

There are many ways these days of establishing a quick and dirty list of potential target numbers. These target companies are often designing their web sites with search engine optimization advisers to ensure they are found by customers!

By inserting this search phase into the process, you give yourself an immediate perspective. You quickly get a feel for the language of certain web sites. You can see how some targets are telling better stories.

You can pick up on crucial topics that targets are covering in their blogs. This gives you great insight into how targets think.

Often this early reconnaissance work will force you to change your Acquisition Profile as the market facts and figures are gathered. Some targets may jump out at you

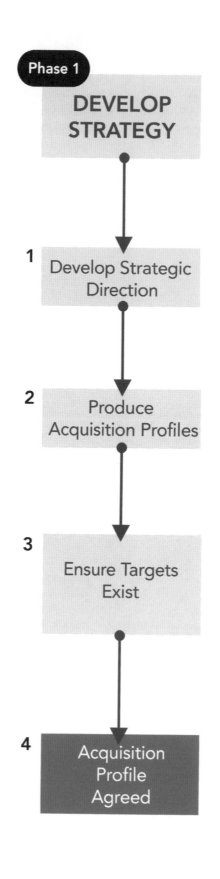

Phase 1

DEVELOP STRATEGY

1 Develop Strategic Direction

2 Produce Acquisition Profiles

3 Ensure Targets Exist

4 Acquisition Profile Agreed

because of their insights. You are building a map of the sector, the people, and the companies. LinkedIn is particularly useful for seeing the connections between people. Connections those people didn't even know they had.

The objective of this stage is not to document every possible target company but instead to clarify that you can expand into this sector knowing that a collection of attractive companies exist. The process is very similar to the approach of world-class sales professionals trying to understand the most likely candidates for their services. From a distance, some sectors look attractive until closer examination reveals a lack of fit.

STAGE 4 – ACQUISITION PROFILE AGREED

It is now possible to sign off on a measured shopping list which reconciles to an attractive strategy with sufficient initial targets. This Acquisition Profile is a powerful document.

Developing Strategy can take weeks or months to get right, but you can see the measured preparation that goes into it. You are forcing management to consider post-acquisition integration and fit with the current core business right out the blocks! Instead of looking all starry eyed at what is for sale, you are ripping the emotion out of the process and focusing on the type of companies that fit well inside your comfort zone and that align with your strategy.

By presenting this type of thinking to the Board, whether it's a large private company, a small, medium, or large public company, or some form of mutual bank, everyone is brought on board.

The Acquisition Approvals Model recognizes a key fact of business. The longer you take to abort from a project, the more expensive the abort costs! You do not want to run an acquisition all the way to due diligence only to find the Group Board isn't behind your thinking.

Influence your team early by conducting rigorous analysis up front. Treat acquisitions as a tool for executing your strategy. This can be hard work, but the odds of the successful integration of target companies are poor. These projects do not have a great track record. However, behind all successful acquirers you will discover a robust process that is relentlessly executed every time. You will see checklists consistently followed. Success with acquisitions comes the hard way – through exceptional preparation.

At the end of every phase of the Acquisition Approvals Model, there is a crucial stage. There is always a sign off. The sign off forces the team to ask the question, do we want to move to the next phase? Sometimes the best decision is to stop and start again, rather than drive forward with the wrong strategy. Assuming sign off occurs, we can now commence Phase 2 – the Identification of Targets.

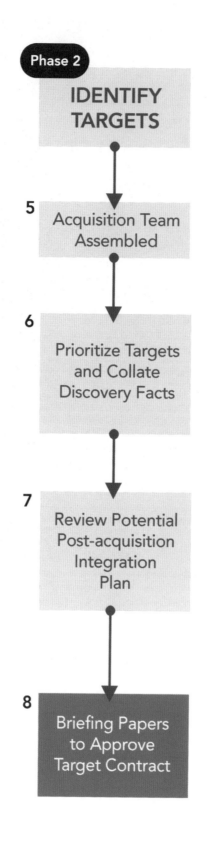

Phase 2

IDENTIFY TARGETS

5 Acquisition Team Assembled

6 Prioritize Targets and Collate Discovery Facts

7 Review Potential Post-acquisition Integration Plan

8 Briefing Papers to Approve Target Contract

Phase 2 – Identify Targets

This phase translates strategy into action. It first defines and then searches for targets that help execute your strategy.

STAGE 5 – ACQUISITION TEAM ASSEMBLED

Successful acquisitions start with "Remarkable Preparation" including grooming the team and setting yourself up for success.

The composition of the team will vary dramatically depending on the size of the acquirer. Many acquisition team members also have day jobs – the financial controller, the internal auditor, the CMO, etc. Ideally the team leader will also be the chief integrator. It's important that post-acquisition integration is built into the thinking as early as possible.

It is worth reviewing with the team some fundamentals:
- Acquisition Profile document.
- Roles of team members.
- How you will process the research of targets.
- Approximate timetable of a deal.
- The overall Acquisition Approvals Model.

Confirm any connections between team members and target companies.

It's worth doing a little scenario planning regarding different types of targets and deal structures using the team.

Have you set up the financing required or set up financing partners subject to the merits of each deal?

Have you rehearsed the big story of why you are growing by acquisition? Can your strategic goals not be met by organic growth? Examples of strong reasons for acquisitions that appeal to all stakeholders, including shareholders, bankers and analysts, include accelerating growth to seize a window of opportunity in the market. This can be driven by specific channel grabs, technology hard to build in-house or entry into new verticals.

Have you listed the priority exposure areas within targets that require early discovery work? E.g., patents, quality of code, types of customers. These typically are deal breakers. Therefore it's worth rehearsing your approach as a team.

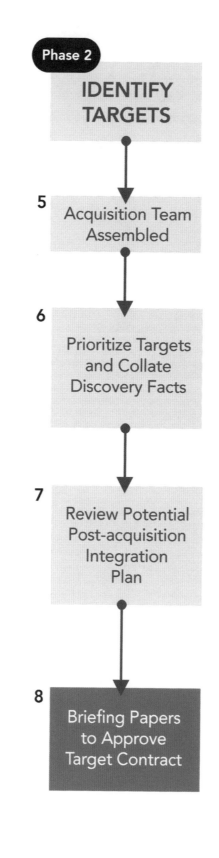

Phase 2

IDENTIFY TARGETS

5 Acquisition Team Assembled

6 Prioritize Targets and Collate Discovery Facts

7 Review Potential Post-acquisition Integration Plan

8 Briefing Papers to Approve Target Contract

This is a great time to remind everyone that acquisitions will only be completed if they assist in executing the company's strategy. It's about being clear as a team what types of targets make sense. You want to establish a robust process to find and churn relevant targets to allow only the highest priority companies to be contacted. This is a hyper-qualification process.

STAGE 6 – PRIORITIZE TARGETS AND COLLATE DISCOVERY FACTS

The M&A tables suggest we are entering a period of frantic deal-making, as busy as the previous high in 2007. However, buying the wrong company can live with you forever. Improve your odds by adopting a professional process for acquisitions.

The key to this phase is finding targets that truly match your Acquisition Profile (shopping list) and being ready to discuss how you would integrate the target into your existing business.

In acquisitions you are constantly worrying about page 10 when you are on page 3! I want you at the end of Phase 2 to be ready to engage in an insightful conversation with a business owner. That takes hard work and homework. You are mimicking post-acquisitio
n integration thinking right now, not once you own the business. As practiced acquirers understand, the aim is to know more about the target than they know about themselves.

Successful acquisitions start with "Remarkable Preparation" including grooming the team and setting yourself up for success.

The acquisition search process has been transformed over the last 10 years as information increasingly comes online. Ideas to find targets include:
- Private Equity portfolios
- Trade shows attendee companies
- Inc. 5000 list
- Software 500 list
- Gartner sector reviews, Hoovers, Keynote, Dunn & Bradstreet, American City Business Journals, Ward's Business Directory
- All sectors/segments have trade bodies with members
- Your own sales teams, technical staff, marketing teams (assuming it is not confidential)
- Influencers, lawyers, accountants, suppliers are all capable of generating ideas

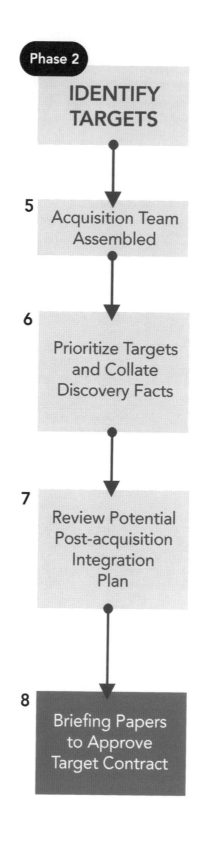

Phase 2

IDENTIFY TARGETS

5 Acquisition Team Assembled

6 Prioritize Targets and Collate Discovery Facts

7 Review Potential Post-acquisition Integration Plan

8 Briefing Papers to Approve Target Contract

COLLATING KEY FACTS - PRACTICAL TIPS

I suggest pulling this together in three strands: market intelligence, target info on people, and all non-people information on the target including financials, products, customers, distribution channels, facilities, etc. Remember this is just the initial gathering of key facts on priority targets. Detailed due diligence covering a plethora of subjects comes later.

Market information should include all the key players, relative size, USPs, key trends, forecasts, threats and opportunities. Ask yourself, what would an investor need to know if you were summarizing the market and the companies within it? What factors are currently undermining your business model?

Target information on each target will vary slightly depending on the sector but needs to include (and this will not be easy for private companies):

- Shareholders
- Sales for the last 5 years
- # of employees
- Profitability
- Main products/services and key business results
- Key customers
- Office locations
- Awards
- Sales channels
- Press Coverage
- Social Media summary
- Estimated market share

As practiced acquirers understand, the aim is to know more about the target than they know about themselves.

People information should include:

- Organization charts
- Bios of the management team
- LinkedIn profiles of key staff
- Google results of key staff
- Technorati ranking of their blogs, twitter rankings, social media ratings

STAGE 7 – REVIEW POTENTIAL POST-ACQUISITION INTEGRATION PLAN

At this stage the team understands the potential acquisition targets within the chosen sectors. Basic information has been gathered and initial prioritization can be placed on the list. In practice, a few targets will stand out.

It may seem too early to be considering how these targets could be integrated into your group, but it isn't. The earlier you consider the hurdles of integration, the better.

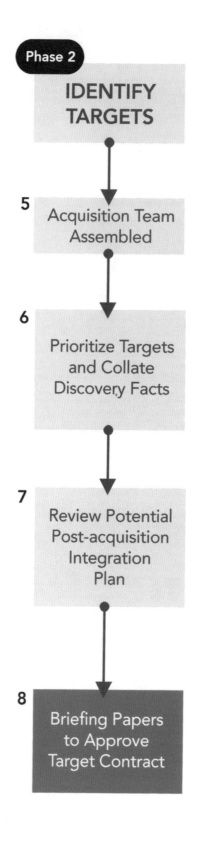

Phase 2

IDENTIFY TARGETS

5 Acquisition Team Assembled

6 Prioritize Targets and Collate Discovery Facts

7 Review Potential Post-acquisition Integration Plan

8 Briefing Papers to Approve Target Contract

Location, the range of products and services, the resumes of key managers, the style of the web site, the customer lists, and much more can be collated to build an early picture of the target.

This view of post-acquisition integration can be a little naïve, depending on how well you know the target from previous interactions, but it is still a valuable exercise to conduct.

This will give you an Engagement Strategy, an angle to engage with the owners of the target. The more insightful and authentic this approach, the higher the probability of success.

For now, you will document the perceived strategic fit with the target and move to the next stage.

STAGE 8 – BRIEFING PAPERS TO APPROVE TARGET CONTACT

Key facts will then be pulled together to allow you to do several things:

1. Assess an initial post-acquisition fit. E.g., there might be immediate client conflict revealed, or geographical fit might be unwieldy.
2. Start to prioritize the target list based on facts, not emotion.
3. Build briefing papers on priority targets seeking a mandate from your Board to contact targets.
4. Craft an insightful script for target contact.

The secret to ending this Phase in a good place is that you have done sufficient homework to understand:

- What value you can bring to the acquisition to grow the business faster.
- The areas of due diligence that you will need to assess before calibrating any deal value.
- Why some companies are more valuable than others – you have perspective.
- Early signs of a cultural fit or not (tip: web sites and blogs give information on the culture of a target).

It's now time to dive into a priority target and engage in a conversation.

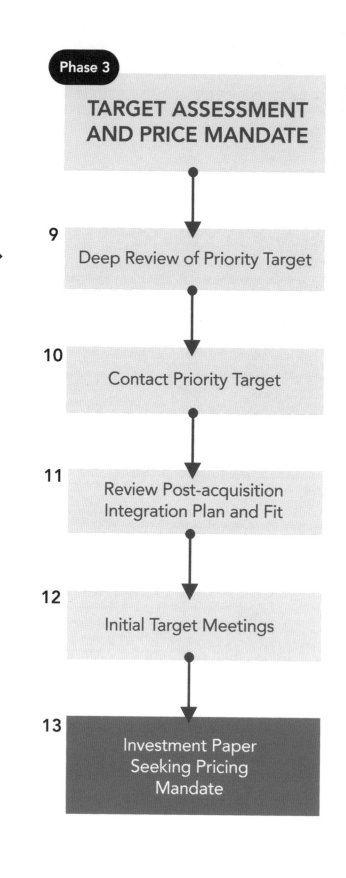

Phase 3

TARGET ASSESSMENT AND PRICE MANDATE

9 Deep Review of Priority Target

10 Contact Priority Target

11 Review Post-acquisition Integration Plan and Fit

12 Initial Target Meetings

13 Investment Paper Seeking Pricing Mandate

Phase 3 – Target Assessment and Price Mandate

In this phase, the emphasis is on assessing value as you get to know the target and translating that into an Investment Paper that articulates your post-acquisition plan. Let's talk about the psychology prior to contacting the target because first impressions matter.

PSYCHOLOGY PRIOR TO CONTACT

The most sensitive subject in this discussion is price. Remembering this tenet will serve you well:

Buyers perceive value, sellers aspire to price.

Each buyer has a unique footprint that they stand in as they assess value. One buyer may have a comprehensive distribution channel and therefore have limited use for the target's sales overhead – think Oracle, IBM, and Baxter. The opposite may be the case where the buyer has no distribution channel and welcomes the target's unique reach into, say, the SMB marketplace and needs the distribution channel. Thus only the buyer, on a case-by-case basis, is capable of calibrating a unique value to them of owning the target business.

The seller on the other hand is aspiring to price. It's not the seller's money that's paying for the deal. The seller might be being influenced by the proceeds her friend achieved from selling her business, or she may be driven by replicating ten years' worth of annual income. She is aspiring!

STAGE 9 – DEEP REVIEW OF PRIORITY TARGET

It seems like hard work—deeply assessing a priority target before you know the owner wants to sell. However, that's the point. No one said that acquisitions were easy. All of the work you've done in Phase 1 and 2 will be brought together by the team with an emphasis on one priority target.

You are about to contact the priority target, so you will create a cheat sheet of the key facts and figures. Think of it as mapping a potential client. You should be able to answer these questions:

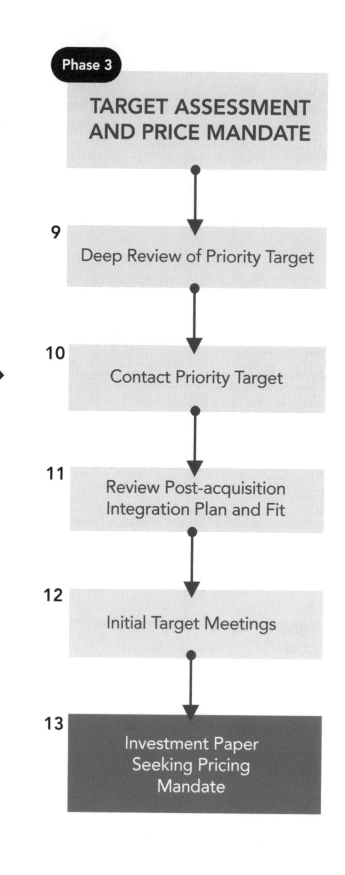

Phase 3

TARGET ASSESSMENT AND PRICE MANDATE

9 Deep Review of Priority Target

10 Contact Priority Target

11 Review Post-acquisition Integration Plan and Fit

12 Initial Target Meetings

13 Investment Paper Seeking Pricing Mandate

1. Who owns the shares?
2. Where do key decision makers and contacts lie within the organizational structure?
3. What are the activities of the target?
4. What market is the target trying to dominate?
5. What is the target's mission statement?
6. Any recent press coverage relevant to this assessment?
7. What is the financial performance of the target? (clearly it's tough getting to up to date financials at this stage, but D&B, Hoovers, Inc. 5000 lists may give a clue)
8. Any change to target's management structure recently?
9. What products do they sell?
10. Who do they sell to?
11. Do they participate in trade shows?
12. Who do they compete against?
13. What job openings do they list?
14. Are they hiring?
15. Why do they say customers should buy from them?
16. Is the target aligned with trade organizations?
17. Does the target have industry certifications? E.g., ISO
18. Are they expanding?
19. Do they distribute internationally?

Each buyer has a unique footprint that they stand in as they assess value

You should also have rehearsed outline integration strategies from total integration to a more stand-alone approach. On first contact be ready to be asked everything from "*How much am I worth?*" to "*How would I fit into your company?*"

STAGE 10 – CONTACT PRIORITY TARGET

There are many bad ways to contact owners of target companies. These include writing anonymous letters claiming to be an interested party either by hiding behind an intermediary or writing directly to the owner. Mysterious voicemails are also a great way to be ignored.

The most effective method is to cold call the owner, principal to principal. This phone call can be made by a close adviser, but the identity of the acquirer needs to be revealed. The owner needs to understand who he or she is dealing with.

Every call is really a meeting. Preparation is everything. What's the objective of the call? What are your big agenda items? What's the ideal outcome? Set out clearly the objective of the call and ask: *does that seem reasonable?* Always clarify a key comment made by the other side.

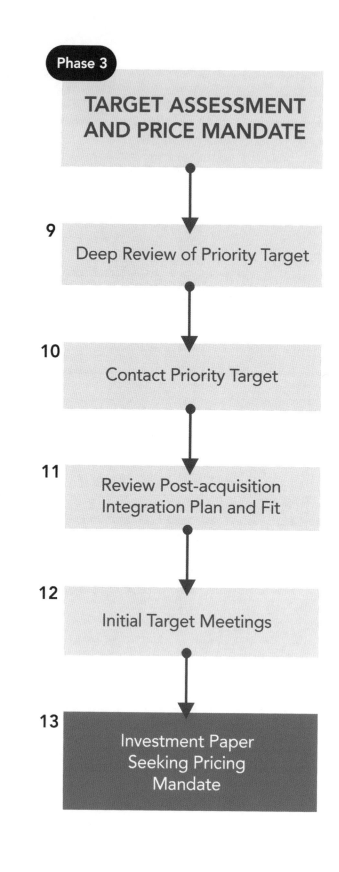

The less you say, the more senior you sound. I hear far too many words being used on calls. I hear answers given to questions never asked. You need to practice shorter sentences and forcing responses. It needs to be a dialogue.

Use non-threatening language. *"We would love to explore a strategic alliance"* is far better than *"We want to buy you."* Don't be sucker-punched into promises you can't keep. You are merely trying to get the "interview" not the "job".

As an alternative, I've seen successful approaches being achieved by a letter. Mail a short, compelling letter to the owner's home address. This should cover the objective of a meeting and the strict confidentiality of any discussions. However, this is a far less successful technique than the power of the human voice explaining with authenticity why an informal chat would be compelling.

If unsuccessful, write to the owners expressing keen interest to follow up if circumstances change at a later date. Assuming this contact is successful, the next step is the acquirer preparing for this first meeting.

STAGE 11 – REVIEW POST-ACQUISITION INTEGRATION PLAN AND FIT

Assuming you've booked the calendar for that first meeting, it's important to put the final touches on preparation.

Pull together all the key facts, and rehearse obvious questions that you will be asked in this first meeting, including your ability to finance a deal, the strategic fit, the post-acquisition plan, the role of the seller's management. Rehearse your answers in a conversational style rather than as answers to a questionnaire!

You will be asked how much you are prepared to pay. Resist this temptation by explaining that you do not possess enough facts to assess value and that a full disclosure of the facts allows acquirers to place a full value on attractive companies.

Acquirers need to send the signal that they are reliable professionals who treat people fairly.

STAGE 12 – INITIAL TARGET MEETINGS

By doing your homework, you are entering these meetings in a relaxed state of mind, but make no mistake, negotiation has begun.

Impress the seller with your knowledge of the market and the seller's competitive positioning in the marketplace.

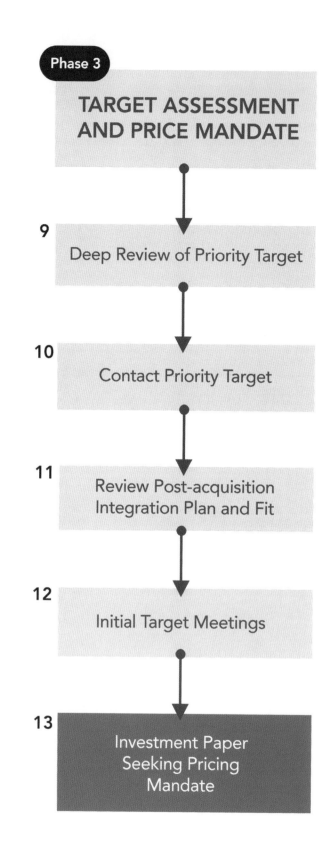

Phase 3

TARGET ASSESSMENT AND PRICE MANDATE

9 Deep Review of Priority Target

10 Contact Priority Target

11 Review Post-acquisition Integration Plan and Fit

12 Initial Target Meetings

13 Investment Paper Seeking Pricing Mandate

Frame the landscape of why you believe there is a fit and your outline thought for growth.

Explain the types of facts you need to gather to assess the potential post-acquisition plan and determine the value to the acquirer of completing a deal.

As a helpful checklist on the essential question of valuation, study the Appendix, *How Much Am I Worth?*

Specific Negotiation Tips:
Negotiation in this environment is not easy. You are discussing someone's lifework. Life is a negotiation. There are a million books on negotiation, but busy executives don't need a book, they need a cheat sheet! I offer these tips based on my experience buying and selling businesses, negotiating with unions, and negotiating with venture capitalists.

These tips are not specific to the first meeting. They relate to all negotiations throughout the entire acquisitions process.

- Always clarify the up-to-date position. E.g., *"You mentioned that a new sales order was imminent the last time we met, tell me more."* Try to establish the housekeeping of the meeting: prospective agenda, time allowed, anyone joining via conference call. This has the subtle advantage of establishing you as de facto chairperson.
- It is essential that your team stay relaxed and focused. Think of the accelerator pedal in your car. If you start the meeting with your foot to the floor you will lose control. You'll get excited, stressed, over-zealous. You will have little emotional capacity to control the car. Stay calm and in control, and seamlessly move up the gears to make a critical point but remember to come back down again.
- Your team leader dictates the pace. Never speak unless invited to do so by the team leader. Don't interrupt a silence. A professional team can make silence look natural.
- Use questions to understand a specific stance. Assumptions can be dangerous. On the other hand, if you are relying on key assumptions in making a point, e.g., the price of a company, state clearly the main facts you believe to be true, including forecasts, to allow yourself an escape route if circumstances change.
- Be yourself, which in my case means **never bluffing**.
- Don't try to be smart. E.g., *"With respect, it is clear from your spreadsheets presented that there is a flaw in your numbers."*
- Watch body language very carefully, especially that of the people not talking.
- Difficult issues should be put to one side to keep the momentum moving forward.
- Use time outs sparingly but effectively to gather your thoughts and garner input from the team.

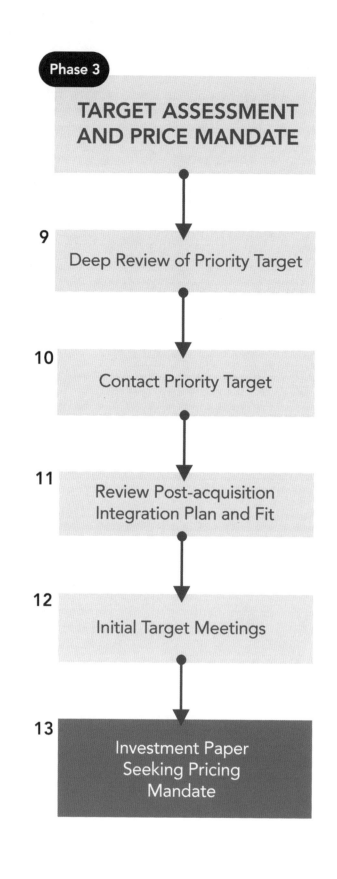

Phase 3

TARGET ASSESSMENT AND PRICE MANDATE

9 Deep Review of Priority Target

10 Contact Priority Target

11 Review Post-acquisition Integration Plan and Fit

12 Initial Target Meetings

13 Investment Paper Seeking Pricing Mandate

- On big points, believe in what you say. It will show.
- If advisers are involved, it is highly recommended that on really big points you deploy the "Principals Only" tactic. E.g., the acquirer and the seller excuse themselves and retreat to a separate room to agree a deal on that essential point.
- The word "help" is underutilized. As in, "*Perhaps you could help me understand how you win the majority of your business.*"
- Rudeness and sarcasm don't work, even if you're British.
- Document agreements along the way and make great theatre of the volume of points agreed.
- Close on clear next steps with a timetable and agree on action for non-compliance.

Negotiation is part art, part science. Try to see the other side's position. If you don't understand it, then ask questions to clarify it. A lack of understanding can blind you to a reasonable stance being taken by the other side.

STAGE 13 – INVESTMENT PAPER SEEKING PRICING MANDATE

The Acquisition Approvals Model demands that critical stages are signed off. Stage 13 is a key stage. You are at a point where you know enough to be dangerous! You've spent some time on the deal, and you've really considered acquiring this company.

The culmination of the first 3 Phases will be a Board Paper seeking a mandate to negotiate a deal. Just forcing your team to write this Board Paper may be enough to stop the process.

This paper allows the Board to review the facts and assess the strategic and financial benefits of a deal. Now is the time to consider leaving the stage, stopping the process professionally and politely rather than at the last minute prior to legal completion.

But if you're sure, then press on. Think of the audience as a cynical non-executive independent director. Contents of the paper?

1. The mandate should articulate the pricing range and key commercial conditions required. Be careful to give yourself some wiggle room. A single price limits your ability to negotiate.
2. Articulate the strategic case for the deal.
3. Set out the logic of the price including:
   - Profits adjusted to reflect your ownership.
   - Multiples used, PE basis, Sales basis, etc.
   - If an earn out deal is proposed, highlight the initial PE and demonstrate that the exit PE is lower when the earn-out is complete.

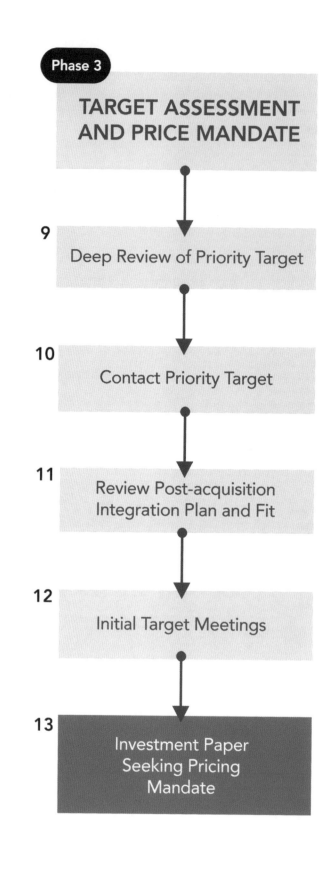

Phase 3

TARGET ASSESSMENT AND PRICE MANDATE

9 Deep Review of Priority Target

10 Contact Priority Target

11 Review Post-acquisition Integration Plan and Fit

12 Initial Target Meetings

13 Investment Paper Seeking Pricing Mandate

- Previous deals done in the industry with prices & multiples paid.
- Highlight specific savings if you are building them into the logic of the deal.
- Highlight the ROI.

By taking this approach, you are dealing with two essential behaviors of successful, practiced acquirers:

- Deciding if you really want to do this deal. Does it make sense? It's much cheaper to exit now rather than later.
- If you want to do this deal, before you enter final negotiations on price, you need to know why you're doing the deal and what it's worth to you.

You will be asked how much you are prepared to pay. Resist this temptation by explaining that you do not possess enough facts to assess value and that a full disclosure of the facts allows acquirers to place a full value on attractive companies.

NEGOTIATE PRICE AND STRUCTURE

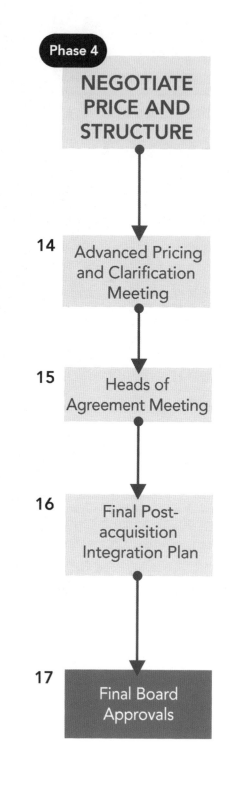

Phase 4

NEGOTIATE PRICE AND STRUCTURE

14 Advanced Pricing and Clarification Meeting

15 Heads of Agreement Meeting

16 Final Post-acquisition Integration Plan

17 Final Board Approvals

Phase 4 – Negotiate Price and Structure

At this stage of an Acquisition you are entering a dangerous phase of emotional attachment. Be careful to continue "auditing the signals." E.g., if the data you uncover makes you uncomfortable don't ignore, but investigate. You have signed off a price mandate with your Board, you have a post-acquisition plan on paper, and now you need to enter this final phase of negotiation confident of the type of deal that works for you.

STAGE 14 – ADVANCED PRICING AND CLARIFICATION MEETING

Prior to a final Heads of Agreement (sometimes called Letter of Intent or Memorandum of Understanding) meeting, I recommend an informal meeting to update on these topics:

1. Latest full year forecasts.
2. Current financial results.
3. New customer wins.
4. New hires or resignations.
5. Assets or shares being purchased.
6. Any exclusions from the sale including assets, subsidiaries, patents.
7. Personal objectives of the seller, price, service contract, role, promises he/she has made to their staff.
8. Market and channel strategies.
9. Status of sales pipeline.
10. Status of cash flow.
11. Any operational issue impacting your post-acquisition plan.

At this stage of an Acquisition you are entering a dangerous phase of emotional attachment.

This is the opportunity to understand the seller's aspirations on price. You may be surprised by how late in the process we are asking the seller about price. But think about what you really know about the target, and think about the timing of your mandate from the Board. I've seen many deals go awry through both sides going after premature pricing.

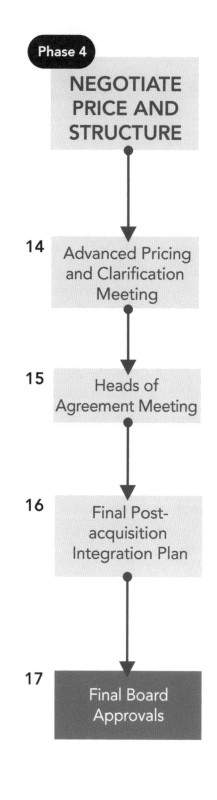

Phase 4

NEGOTIATE PRICE AND STRUCTURE

14 Advanced Pricing and Clarification Meeting

15 Heads of Agreement Meeting

16 Final Post-acquisition Integration Plan

17 Final Board Approvals

It's really only at this point in the process that you have close to a full picture of the target. It's only with this level of knowledge that you have been able to get approval from the Board to negotiate. Now you can discuss price with perspective.

It's essential to deploy the negotiations tips for target meetings (Stage 12). Pricing and clarification meetings are often tense. They require a calm head and hyper-vigilant awareness of mood and timing.

Take time-outs when needed, but don't overuse them.

Assuming you have a meeting of minds and that all the key facts are understood, then I recommend booking calendars for a formal Heads of Agreement Meeting within the next two weeks. This gives the acquirer a chance to revisit the logic, the price, the structure, and the post-acquisition integration plan of this specific deal.

STAGE 15 – HEADS OF AGREEMENT MEETING

This meeting is an opportunity to finalize the terms and conditions of the deal. Terms signed off in this meeting will form the basis of legal contracts. The agenda and order of events are important.

I suggest the following:
1. Update since last meeting: it is vital to clarify even at this late stage any change of information which affects the deal. Dramatic events can hit a business just prior to a Heads of Agreement.
2. Confirmation of what is included: it is possible that misunderstandings still exist, especially relating to private assets of the owners, e.g., the Aston Martin.
3. Earn-out formula and period: too often in deals, due to time pressure or other reasons, earn-out deals are not clarified in sufficient detail through worked examples.
4. IP: acquirers must ensure that the relevant IP is owned by the target company and not by individuals or companies outside the target group.
5. Key employees should be discussed and their future roles explained.
6. Removal of personal guarantees: the removal of these guarantees should be sold as a benefit of the deal but are often overlooked.
7. Necessary warranties and indemnities: although an issue to be discussed in detail at the contract stage, it is a great opportunity to spell out the key ones the buyer will expect to see in place.
8. Purchase price and consideration: Keep this down the agenda until you have achieved some momentum to the meeting. I will merely add this thought to previous thoughts on pricing—you should adopt a "no regrets" policy. You do not want to lose the deal by low-balling only to see a competitor close the deal at a price you thought fair! On the other hand, if the business is worth $30.5m to you, then that's it.

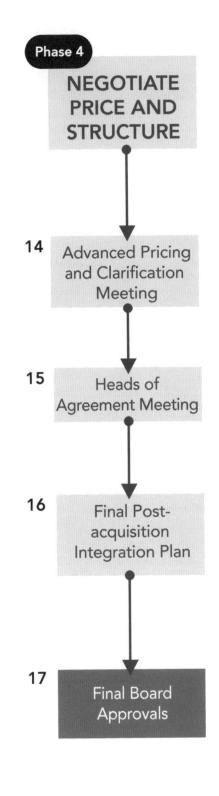

Phase 4

NEGOTIATE PRICE AND STRUCTURE

14 Advanced Pricing and Clarification Meeting

15 Heads of Agreement Meeting

16 Final Post-acquisition Integration Plan

17 Final Board Approvals

Be careful that the seller has a mandate to represent all sellers. There is no point if a majority shareholder agrees a deal but his brother owning, say, 30% of the company is not in the room and not on the same page.

This meeting is all about selling the benefits of being acquired by the acquirer. When you're buying, you're selling. In the end, sellers are clearly influenced by the money, but they are often (not always) concerned about the treatment of their people, especially if some of their staff are family members.

Be careful that the seller has a mandate to represent all sellers.

Exclusivity is important. As an acquirer you want to establish an exclusivity or lock-out period to allow due diligence to take place without a competitive threat. Eight weeks is an acceptable exclusivity period to completion.

The order of the agenda is important. When an impasse is reached on a point, learn to park it and come back to it later. Establish some rapport early on and focus on what is agreed. Don't rush to explore the details of the earn-out if the up-front figure is still not agreed.

As a team, speak with one voice. All members of the team need to follow the lead negotiator. As stated earlier, always be ready to call a time-out when needed but don't overuse it.

The Heads of Agreement meeting should conclude with the acquirer promising to send out the formal summary document to be signed by both sides.

Before leaving the subject of Heads of Agreement, I want to give some practical commercial advice on Earn-Outs.

EARN-OUTS

When Genzyme announced in 2011 that it was exploring a new deal structure to help resolve the impasse on price with bidder Sanofi-Aventis, it highlighted a great tool in the M&A world, the earn-out deal. They called the structure a CVR, or Contingent Value Right, an earn-out by another name. The seller receives further consideration beyond the amount paid at completion dependent on certain targets being met.

The Philosophy of Earn-Out deals: The concept is quite simple. The buyer's perception of value is lower than the seller's aspiration on price. This gap is usually fueled by differing views on the potential growth of the target company.

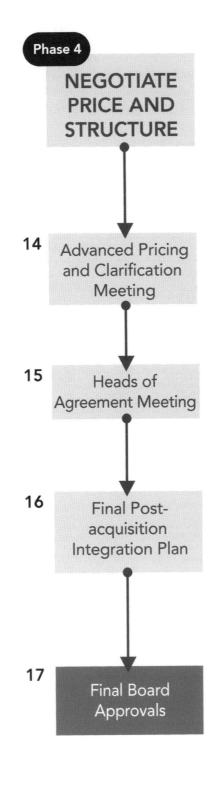

Phase 4

NEGOTIATE PRICE AND STRUCTURE

14 Advanced Pricing and Clarification Meeting

15 Heads of Agreement Meeting

16 Final Post-acquisition Integration Plan

17 Final Board Approvals

In Genzyme's case, the gap revolved around the future revenue stream of Campath, a multiple sclerosis drug. Genzyme projected that sales would reach $3.5 billion in 2017; the buyer believed more like $700m! There you have it, the future value gap. The earn-out attempts to wrap a formula around that gap (could be profits, gross profits, sales) and pay outs are based on achievement of predictions being achieved.

These techniques were famously used to build up large service groups, e.g., WPP, the world's largest advertising agency. There is an important negotiation point worth stating. The earn-out amount is in addition to the up front sum paid to gain 100% of the shares. The earn-out doesn't buy the buyer any more shares. The 100% of shares are bought by the up front sum with a contractual agreement to pay more if relevant conditions are met. That means if you are an owner of a company, private or public, you expect the buyer to show full respect for what the target has achieved to date, within the up front sum. The battle of minds should be around a fair price for today's achievement, and therefore earn-outs should relate to incremental performance beyond today. This seems obvious, but often these facts are lost in the emotion of deals.

Structuring Earn-Outs: A worked example is always easier to understand. Private selling company Smith Inc. has produced EBITDA of $10m during the previous financial year, and their 3-year forecasts suggest future profits of $12m, $13m and $16m as new products come on stream. The following structure attempts to produce a win:win. The seller gets full respect for results to date but also some more upside if the business delivers the forecasts. From a buyer's perspective, the deal looks attractive and safe.

- Pay $117m which looks fair at EBITDA multiple of 11.7 but structured as:

  - Up front $80m, EBITA multiple of 8 times historical earning
  - Earn-out formula 10 times (average of projections > $10m) e.g.
    10 ($13.67m-$10m) = $37m

- Total consideration if targets are met, $80m plus $37m = $117m but you own a business producing $16m profit

- Initial EBITDA multiple = 8, Exit multiple (when you have stopped paying) 7.3

I'll deal with the rules for earn-outs to be included in the Purchase and Sale Agreement below at Stage 20.

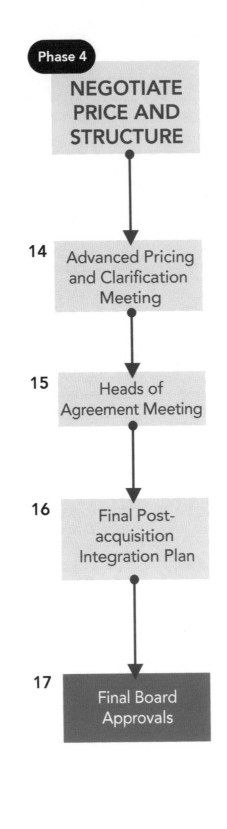

Phase 4

NEGOTIATE PRICE AND STRUCTURE

14 Advanced Pricing and Clarification Meeting

15 Heads of Agreement Meeting

16 Final Post-acquisition Integration Plan

17 Final Board Approvals

STAGE 16 – FINAL POST-ACQUISITION INTEGRATION PLAN

Let's remember the research from the introduction. Most research done points to around 50% of acquisitions being a failure in the eyes of the acquirer. Research conducted by Cass Business School, covering 12,339 deals including 2,917 acquisitions of distressed companies from 1984 to 2008, concludes that price is not the determining factor for success but that post-acquisition integration is the key (Moeller).

That puts post-acquisition integration at the top of the agenda.

So, at this stage, just prior to full approval from the Board to commit to commercial and legal due diligence, it is important to review your post-acquisition integration plan.

This will shape both your approach to due diligence and the actions required in the days after completion of the deal. You've gathered considerable facts on the target at this stage, and you need to validate that the post-acquisition plan still makes sense.

Distribution plans, managers' roles, location of facilities, equipment needed, funding of the target, all need to be scrutinized based on the facts before you. A specific checklist is offered at Stage 22 below.

STAGE 17 – FINAL BOARD APPROVALS

This is an important final approvals phase. It's the reason medical staff, airline pilots, and project managers have checklists. It's the final review by the acquisition team. It's a chance to review all facts and figures and list all concerns. It gives the acquiring Board the opportunity to sanction the deal subject to due diligence and contract.

The acquisition team should take this opportunity to specify the exact nature and scope of due diligence.

Of course, the acquirer should also take the opportunity to clarify that the seller has all approvals in place as well.

The acquirer should have in place an exclusivity agreement covering the next eight weeks. It's not acceptable for the seller to be shopping the deal around at the same time as the acquirer is investing significant capital into due diligence. Often, both parties negotiate a reasonable break-up fee which, if the seller changes their mind, is payable by the seller to the buyer to compensate for wasted time and money.

DUE DILIGENCE AND LEGAL AGREEMENTS

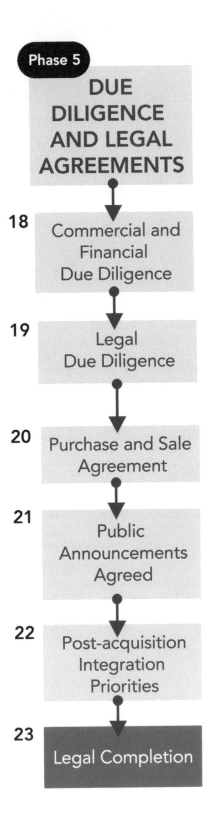

Phase 5

DUE DILIGENCE AND LEGAL AGREEMENTS

18 Commercial and Financial Due Diligence

19 Legal Due Diligence

20 Purchase and Sale Agreement

21 Public Announcements Agreed

22 Post-acquisition Integration Priorities

23 Legal Completion

Phase 5 – Due Diligence and Legal Agreements

At the end of this phase, you will own the target company. Therefore it's worth considering the real objectives of due diligence, both commercial and legal.

So here is the issue to consider – are you focusing all your efforts on validating the past? Are you auditing the financial statements, the inventory, accounting records, HR records, capital structure, etc., at the expense of validating the future? Are you validating your post-acquisition integration plan?

You have a limited timeframe to complete your due diligence, and of course you need to validate the state of the business. However, you also need to validate your post-acquisition integration plan. The acquisition integration team will make assumptions in order to build a plan. Those assumptions need to form part of the due diligence (both commercial & legal) checklist. Here are my top 10 assumptions worth validating when an earn-out is involved:

TOP 10 ASSUMPTIONS
1. The owners understandably want to stay, e.g., attractive earn-out, bigger role, access to capital to scale.

2. All key customers will come across with the deal and find the buyer acceptable.

3. There are no conflicts of interest between the seller's customer list and the buyer's list.

4. All equipment deployed in the business is sustainable and does not require upgrade in the short term.

5. Monthly financial routines will allow seamless integration with the buyer's reporting requirements.

6. As acquirer, you will be able to sell the seller's products through your distribution network (and if relevant, you can sell your products through the seller's network).

7. You understand how you will integrate the differing sales commission plans between both sides.

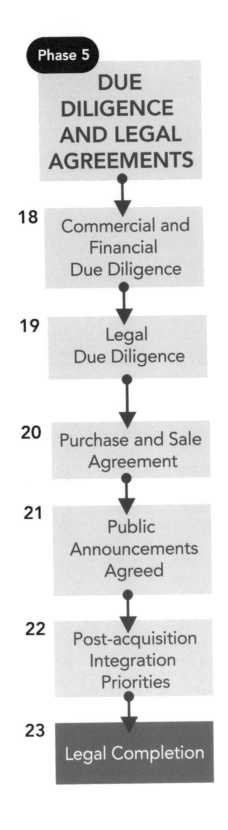

Phase 5

DUE DILIGENCE AND LEGAL AGREEMENTS

18 Commercial and Financial Due Diligence

19 Legal Due Diligence

20 Purchase and Sale Agreement

21 Public Announcements Agreed

22 Post-acquisition Integration Priorities

23 Legal Completion

8. The commercial salaries and bonuses you will offer the sellers and the key managers post completion are acceptable.

9. The rules surrounding the earn-out are practical and allow the buyer complete latitude to manage the business.

10. The next 12 months under your ownership is reflected in a motivational business plan including monthly cash flow forecasts.

STAGE 18 – COMMERCIAL & FINANCIAL DUE DILIGENCE

With of all that said, let's tackle due diligence in two parts. The first part is commercial and financial due diligence. As an acquirer, it is important to be disciplined and focused on the areas you want to cover, given the limited time available. A reasonable timeframe to complete due diligence for most private company acquisitions would be six to eight weeks but could be longer depending on the complexity of the business.

From the seller's position, it is important to build a virtual data room of key documents in an easy to access system. There are many specific apps on the market in 2015 to assist in this process including software like Dropbox or a more sophisticated content management system such as SharePoint.

Therefore, the acquirer needs to investigate all operational areas of the business to confirm the deal still makes sense. As a checklist, ensure you cover:

1. History & description of business
   - History & development
   - Group organization, company structure
   - Statistical information
   - Capital structure (including shareholder agreements)
   - Corporate Objectives

2. Management & employees
   - Management structure
   - Directors and senior management
   - Employees
   - Earnings policies
   - Staff and labor relations

3. Accounting records & management information
   - Financial accounting records
   - Costing systems

- Key performance indicators
- IT systems
- Budgets
- Foreign Exchange Management
- Forecasting
- Board Packs
- Audited statements

4. Marketing
   - Main product lines
   - Main markets
   - Customers
   - Distribution methods
   - Terms of Trade
   - Competitors and their products
   - Campaigns
   - Market analysis reports
   - Social media strategy
   - Metrics measured
   - Web site platform & structure

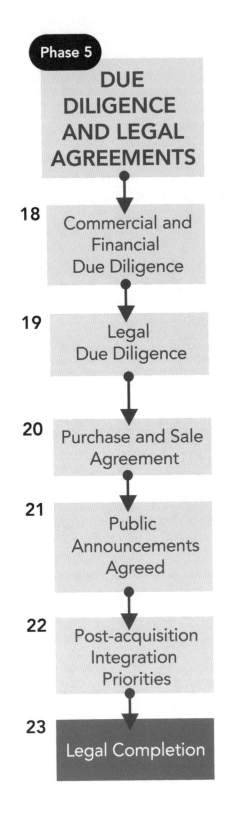

Phase 5

DUE DILIGENCE AND LEGAL AGREEMENTS

18 Commercial and Financial Due Diligence

19 Legal Due Diligence

20 Purchase and Sale Agreement

21 Public Announcements Agreed

22 Post-acquisition Integration Priorities

23 Legal Completion

5. Production & purchasing
    *   Production strategy
    *   Existing production facilities and current usage
    *   Manufacturing efficiency
    *   Future requirements
    *   Purchasing organization
    *   Purchasing policy
    *   R&D Strategy
    *   Product Road Maps
    *   Environmental Matters

6. Assets & Liabilities
    *   Fixed assets details
    *   Leases
    *   Investments
    *   Stock details
    *   Accounts receivables
    *   Aged listings
    *   Borrowings
    *   Litigation
    *   401k details

7. All legal contracts, employee employment contracts, bonus structures, Long Term Incentive Plans, Shareholder Agreements, need to be reviewed.

8. Taxation
    *   Returns
    *   Payroll Records

So here is the issue to consider — are you focusing all your efforts on validating the past?... Are you validating your post-acquisition integration plan?

STAGE 19 & 20 – LEGAL DUE DILIGENCE AND AGREEMENTS

The second part of due diligence is the legal review. Use these guidelines as you work alongside your legal team.

Walk through every detail of the Heads of Agreement and the findings of the due diligence exercise. Ensure that all commercial terms are meticulously covered by the Purchase & Sale Agreement, specifically with regard to concerns raised by the due diligence exercise. Assuming these are not price adjustment issues, ensure you have appropriate warranties and indemnities to mitigate your risk.

The purpose of warranties and indemnities is primarily to flush out disclosures. E.g., Buyer wants a warranty that there are likely no bad debts in Accounts Receivable. The seller agrees to the warranty but discloses the exception that, say, a customer called Smith & Jones based in Japan owes seller $23,000 but they have provided fully against it in the bad debt provision.

If an earn-out structure is involved, buyer must ensure the contract includes a real worked example illustrating the formula. The meaning of an earn-out is often mangled when written in legalese!

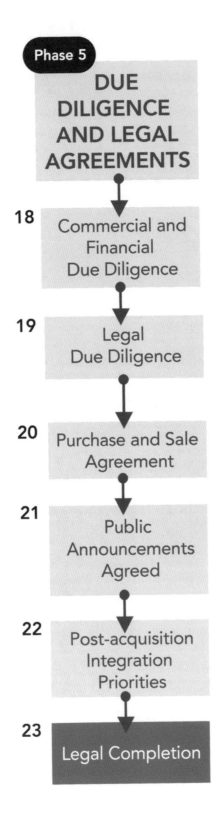

Phase 5

DUE DILIGENCE AND LEGAL AGREEMENTS

18 Commercial and Financial Due Diligence

19 Legal Due Diligence

20 Purchase and Sale Agreement

21 Public Announcements Agreed

22 Post-acquisition Integration Priorities

23 Legal Completion

Legal contracts often have a dozen essential themes written into them. As the principal leading the deal, make sure your attorney explains the key ones to win. There is no such thing as a legal point, merely commercial ones!

Don't offend anyone by including boilerplate clauses in the contract that are not relevant to the deal.

As the acquirer, **you** prepare the Purchase & Sale Agreement and stay in control.

Earn-Out Rules to document: When earn-outs are being executed, remember, the buyer is buying 100% of the target. The buyer has full control of the business on day 1. Therefore, it is important that sellers build protections into the Purchase contract. You can expect sellers to want a discussion on:

- Accounting policies to be used.
- Management charges from the buyer, e.g., payroll, legal, treasury services.
- Intra group pricing to be deployed.
- Cost of finance provided by the buyer.
- The appointment of auditors.
- Rules concerning changes to staff.

The objective of these rules is to avoid arguments post-acquisition. Imagine the post-acquisition strategy, and legislate for the obvious.

ISSUES TO NEGOTIATE

1. Earn-outs do not work in every case. If you intend to totally integrate the acquired company from day 1, earn-outs around profits are impossible.
2. Remember an earn-out effectively ring fences a target company until the deal is paid out. Gross margin & sales earn-outs do allow some integration post-acquisition.
3. Salaries can't be artificially held down by the seller to pump up profits.
4. When things go wrong, don't hang around; post-acquisition, move in and fix the problem.
5. Long earn-out deals never work. The recommended max time for earn-outs is three years but probably better with two. The sales earn-out can be longer if the revenue stream can be kept separate.

STAGE 21 – PUBLIC ANNOUNCEMENTS AGREED

These can vary dramatically depending on the size and nature of the deal. The seller's wishes to keep price and other details out of the spotlight will drive the content. Regulatory demands will clearly influence what needs to be said.

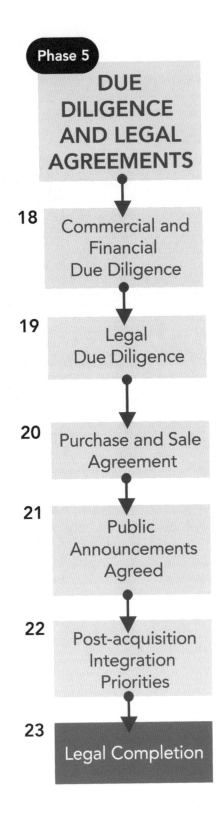

Phase 5

DUE DILIGENCE AND LEGAL AGREEMENTS

18 Commercial and Financial Due Diligence

19 Legal Due Diligence

20 Purchase and Sale Agreement

21 Public Announcements Agreed

22 Post-acquisition Integration Priorities

23 Legal Completion

Remember to consider the employees of both sides. On the seller's side, it is inevitable that many long-term employees will not see an immediate financial benefit to the deal. They see their fellow colleagues, bosses, and family members who are shareholders walking away with millions of dollars. This is as much a problem of motivation for the buyer as the seller. The last thing the buyer needs is a demotivated set of employees under their ownership.

How will you handle key customers? I recommend the acquirer and the seller meet with key customers together to explain the logic of the deal and why it will result in improved outcomes for the customer.

This is also a great opportunity to draft a joint press release announcing the deal. The beauty of dealing with these announcements in a relaxed atmosphere is that there is time to tweak the language and to get the announcements approved by both Boards.

Make no mistake—the story of the deal is important. There are many stakeholders to a deal. Employees, shareholders, suppliers, customers, prospects, bankers, prospective job candidates, and regulators all have a take on what the deal means to them. The story of the deal should be an exciting, compelling event that makes sense to all parties and is motivating to employees.

Take time to reach out to the seller's senior management to clarify their roles post-acquisition, your strategy for the future, your vision for the sector, and the potential for career enhancement going forward.

STAGE 22 – POST-ACQUISITION INTEGRATION PRIORITIES

This Playbook has emphasized from the start the importance of post-acquisition integration. Now, all the planning needs to come together into a prioritized to-do list with names assigned who own the tasks.

The mindset is simple. The mindset for integration is to consider the fact you are about to add a material number of employees to each of your departments.

The complete stand alone acquisition is out of the question. You are about to onboard another 10, 20 ,200, or 2000 new employees and integrate them into your corporate structure. The more you think like that, the more your post-acquisition integration plan will succeed. The following checklist should help you cover the basics:

SALES DEPARTMENT
- Anomalies between acquirer and target sales commissions will require urgent action as sales teams talk.
- Onboarding new customers

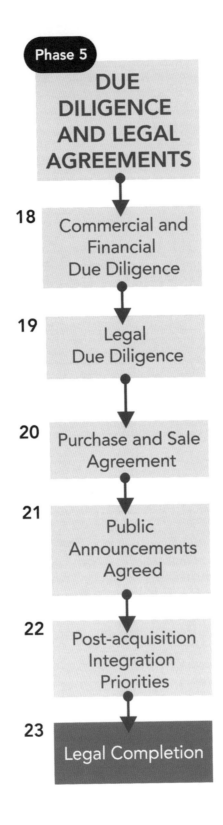

Phase 5

DUE DILIGENCE AND LEGAL AGREEMENTS

18 Commercial and Financial Due Diligence

19 Legal Due Diligence

20 Purchase and Sale Agreement

21 Public Announcements Agreed

22 Post-acquisition Integration Priorities

23 Legal Completion

- Reconciling sales process
- Merging CRM systems
- Organize immediate training related to closing sales and keeping customers happy.
- Ensure live deals under negotiation are not disrupted by the acquisition.
- Cleanse all sales forecasts ASAP and integrate the revised version into the group cash forecasting system.
- Review cross selling opportunities between key customers of buyer and seller.

Practical Points to Consider

I would urge caution when consolidating commission plans. If your post-acquisition plan calls for the integration of the target's sales force into the acquirer's sales force, you have no choice but to consider this problem. Moving too quickly to standardize commission plans can demotivate huge chunks of your team because you've just effectively announced a pay cut. Take your time working out motivational incentives for your newly-acquired talent. Give them the opportunity to make more money if they are successful. If rationalization is necessary, be compassionate and offer out-placement services if possible. Where the target's sales team is being left in place (perhaps because of an earn-out deal structure), you must allow the target's CEO to manage those incentives and to implement a new plan relevant for the circumstances.

FINANCE DEPARTMENT

- Get control of the bank accounts, including check signatories and authorization limits.
- Ensure all accounts are receiving the best group interest rate now that the target is part of a larger entity.
- Establish operating budgets including capex with authorization guidelines.
- Establish a new management information report timetable. In the early stages of integration – metrics will be key.
- Review balance sheets for adequacy of provisions.
- Drive through planned cost savings quickly and effectively with clear communication. Demonstrate leadership.
- Tax and accounting matters related to regulatory compliance may require urgent action.

The mindset for integration is to consider the fact you are about to add a material number of employees to each of your departments.

Practical Points to Consider

You own the business, and you need to own the financial governance of the target. The mistake that is often made is to assume that the acquirer's forecasting

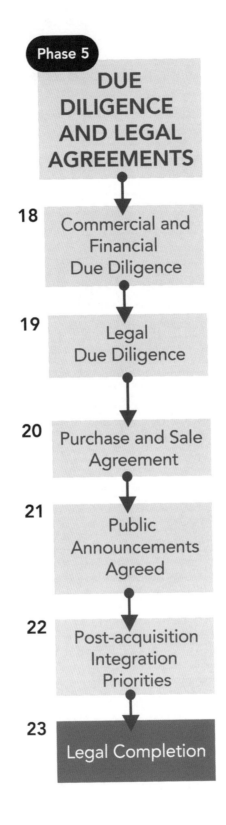

Phase 5

DUE DILIGENCE AND LEGAL AGREEMENTS

18 Commercial and Financial Due Diligence

19 Legal Due Diligence

20 Purchase and Sale Agreement

21 Public Announcements Agreed

22 Post-acquisition Integration Priorities

23 Legal Completion

model is far superior to the target's model. That could be a big mistake. The target's management team has built an attractive business using smart metrics and forecasting models. Assess these carefully before imposing your controls and systems. Of course, you need essential information for consolidation purposes, but this doesn't mean fixing something that isn't broken.

TARGET LEADERSHIP
- Establish a reporting structure to ensure continued trading is seamless.
- Review reward structures to ensure continuity of management, especially if an earn-out excludes some key people.
- Do a quick and dirty review of problem employment contracts, and put resolutions in place to minimize exposure.
- Establish a key meetings schedule to allow free and timely flow of information.
- Establish a clear understanding of the authority levels of the target's leadership team.

Practical Points to Consider

During the negotiation phase of a deal, it's important to remember that you will have to live with consequences of creating bad blood. It may sound dramatic, but I've seen countless situations where the target CEO completes the deal for the money but is on a mission to get even after the deal is closed. So, handling post-acquisition leadership talent actually starts way before the deal closes. The way you interact with the target owners/management prior to legal completion matters. People remember how they were treated. Now, assuming you've handled that well and built up trust, the next action is to deliver on your promises. The senior executive on the acquirer's side that was appointed to make the acquisition a success must communicate often to ensure both sides are executing on the plan. Leadership of the target needs clarity. They have new bosses, and they need to understand what's expected of them.

IT DEPARTMENT
- Deal with exposures revealed by due diligence, prioritizing those related to keeping the trains running!
- Articulate an operational plan for merging disparate systems, or at least to allow them to "talk" to each other.
- Lock down the security around customer databases to ensure recently departed staff can't access vital information.

Practical Points to Consider

Disparate systems need to talk to each other. You will have identified the problem areas during due diligence, and now is the time to execute your plan. Like any good project plan, it needs five essential ingredients: a project leader, agreement of the issues, resources of people and money required, objectives and deadlines. Every

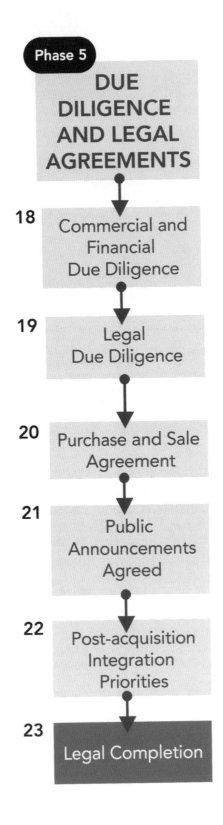

Phase 5

DUE DILIGENCE AND LEGAL AGREEMENTS

18 Commercial and Financial Due Diligence

19 Legal Due Diligence

20 Purchase and Sale Agreement

21 Public Announcements Agreed

22 Post-acquisition Integration Priorities

23 Legal Completion

deal is different. Treat each situation with respect, and you will be fine. Patience and diplomacy will be required in spades!

MARKETING DEPARTMENT

- Communicate often and clearly with staff and key external stakeholders, especially key customers.
- Visit key customers to articulate the strategy of the merged group and why it's good news for that customer. (An overview version of this should have been done during commercial and financial due diligence.)
- The sellers will have signed off on the joint press release on the deal. This is a great opportunity to motivate staff and impress existing customers with the correct tone of message.
- Set a timetable for all web site changes and allocate a webmaster to drive the project.
- Collateral may need to change to reflect the new products of the merged entity.
- Don't miss the opportunity to articulate the enhanced business result that will be achieved for your customers due to the increased resources of the merged group.

Practical Points to Consider

Write and re-write the story of the deal until it's crisp and makes sense to a 6th grader. Don't overpromise on synergies. They will crucify you later as you're asked to comment on your performance relative to those promises. Look at the story you are telling through the eyes of your key customers (especially those of the target). Is this deal good news for them?

LEGAL DEPARTMENT

- Draw up a detailed checklist of leases, obligations, trade contracts, employment contracts, IPR, and change of control provisions, and articulate any commercial issues that require decisions by the leadership team.
- Note that if an earn-out formed part of the deal, there may be quite onerous conditions regarding managing the newly acquired company. These will need to be factored into the integration plan.
- Insurance and risk exposure reviews should be conducted as a high priority.

Practical Points to Consider

Structure your actions into 30, 60, and 90-day timetables. Some stuff must happen immediately, e.g., insurance exposure or commercial issues that could harm the business. Pension and 401k issues may take longer because approvals are needed.

Overall, the key message is to be prepared and to execute the integration with confidence. The worst thing you can do is to procrastinate. Make your acquisitions

Phase 5

DUE DILIGENCE AND LEGAL AGREEMENTS

18 Commercial and Financial Due Diligence

19 Legal Due Diligence

20 Purchase and Sale Agreement

21 Public Announcements Agreed

22 Post-acquisition Integration Priorities

23 Legal Completion

a success. And remember—nothing succeeds as planned, but failing to plan is planning to fail.

STAGE 23 – LEGAL COMPLETION

The formal legal completion can be a restrained event or more of a celebration. Each deal is different. There may still be some late drafting changes to the Purchase and Sale Agreement requiring negotiation.

It always amazes me how many pieces of paper appear at these meetings requiring signature. Last minute approvals may be delayed, and I've certainly been in 24-hour sessions to get the deal signed by 5pm on the anointed day!

As always, patience is key. There are almost always surprises at these events. I remember on a small deal, the seller seemed to be changing his mind. Suddenly he left the room and was gone. His adviser assured us that this was normal. This was how he handled the big events in his life. He needed to walk it off and be alone. It was at least 50 minutes of angst before he appeared back in the room ready to sign!

Sometimes the seller chooses this last moment to deliver copious disclosures. These are a collection of admissions designed to undermine the effectiveness of the warranties built into the agreement.

Each and every disclosure needs to be read, analyzed, and put into plain English by the legal team. Often, these disclosures are reasonable exceptions and one-off events that have no material bearing on the deal. These could include a junior employee leaving, a minor customer not renewing a contract, or a minor change to an internal policy.

As soon as the deal completes, it is time to execute the meeting with the seller's employees to formally announce the deal. Tactics will vary depending on the relative size of the deal. Town Hall type meetings, if practical, can be very effective at delivering a timely, clear story of the logic of the deal. Videos might be appropriate where multiple locations are involved. There will be numerous smaller meetings involving senior management as the weeks go by. The secret is to over-communicate as, left unchecked, fear, uncertainty, and doubt will always fill the void..

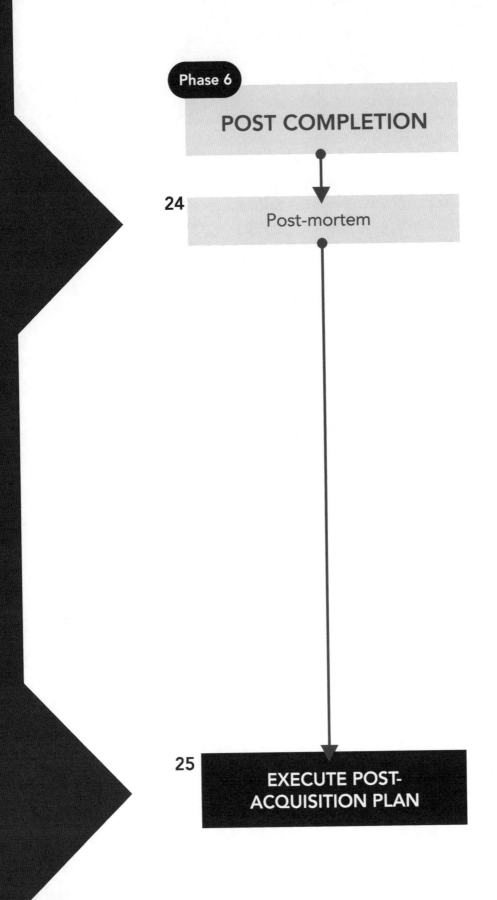

Phase 6

POST COMPLETION

24 Post-mortem

25 EXECUTE POST-ACQUISITION PLAN

Phase 6 – Post Completion

STAGE 24 – POST-MORTEM

Really practiced acquirers understand the importance of the post-mortem. They understand it's not about the number of deals you do. It's about *what you learn* from each deal. It's about the lessons learned from every deal. It's not just about understanding why certain deals were aborted, but also what went wrong and what worked in *successful* completions.

It's essential to hold post-mortems after each deal. I can't emphasize this enough! An import research study by Dr. Koen H. Heimeriks, Stephen Gates, and Maurizo Zollo pointed out that:

> Maintaining a body of M&A knowledge, organizing it into lessons and making it easily accessible are key to developing and leveraging a company's M&A capability. Without such a framework, companies can slip into applying general types of strategies developed in prior acquisitions that are inappropriate to the one in hand. Managers might also become overconfident by thinking that the mere accumulation of experience brings with it a stronger capability.
>
> ("The Secrets of Successful Acquisitions")

I recommend reviewing the performance of the acquisition team immediately after legal completion because memories are fresh. The consequences of mistakes are clear. Major issues should force changes to your version of the Acquisition Approvals Model. Perhaps you need to prepare better for meetings. Perhaps you need to uncover pension issues earlier. Perhaps you need to work better together as a team.

STAGE 25 – EXECUTE POST-ACQUISITION PLAN

Finally, the success of the deal will rely on the execution of post-acquisition integration. This should be driven by the head of integration—one point person charged with making integration a success. That project manager should drive the plan by conducting regular review meetings of the integration team.

The integration team needs to include representatives from the original seller's team. Remember, you are all on the same side now.

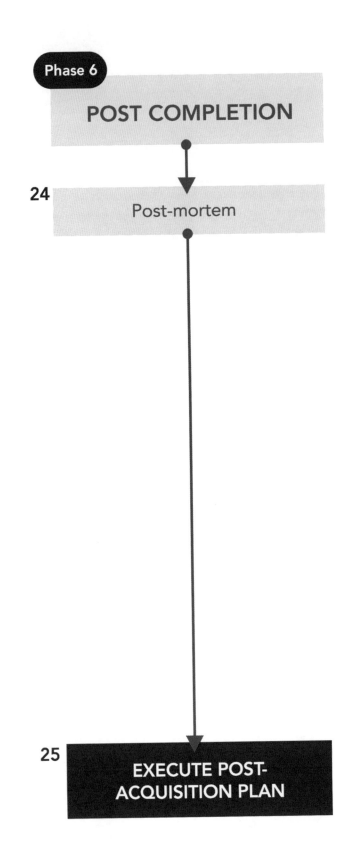

Phase 6

POST COMPLETION

24 Post-mortem

25 EXECUTE POST-ACQUISITION PLAN

As a final thought on integration, it's worth covering one key aspect, *the culture problem*. These considerations should form part of your thinking throughout The Acquisition Approvals Process.

THE CULTURE PROBLEM

- In due diligence, try to really understand how the target company operates day to day. How the company forecasts their sales pipeline, how they win business, hold meetings, reward staff. Try to imagine how your own culture would operate within this business. Is there a stark and glaring mismatch? If so, maybe you need to walk away.

- Don't be blind to a better way of doing things. The target might have a better, slicker sales process, forecasting system, a better hiring machine, a better new product development team. Ask yourself, how am I going to protect the good stuff that I want to nurture under my ownership?

- Owners leave businesses they sell. Why does that need to be the case? Over the last 16 years or so, Google has been a prolific acquirer. Their batting average? Approximately 67% of CEOs stay after the acquisition. Google clearly thinks through how to keep the ex- owner motivated, and I suspect it worries about the cultural fit more than most.

- Treat every acquisition on a case-by-case basis. Don't have a one-size fits all approach to integration. Some acquisitions might be a technology grab, saving you years of development. You clearly would approach cultural integration on that deal differently from the acquisition of a consultancy business.

- It might make sense to have an earn-out form part of the deal structure. This will limit your ability to fully integrate the target, but you are trading that off with the advantages of the earn-out structure. Often the rules of the earn-out will prevent the acquirer from materially changing the way the target is run and, indirectly, the culture within the target.

- When you are buying, you are selling. Don't miss opportunities as an acquirer to switch on the target's senior management to your brand, your success, and your ability to develop talent. Remember the research on why people come to work (See Daniel Pink's great book, *Drive*):

    - Autonomy—the ability and freedom to own and do their job.
    - Mastery—understanding that people want to get better at what they do.
    - Purpose—staff want to understand how their role fits into the big picture.

    These are things acquirers can be really good at but often are silent on.

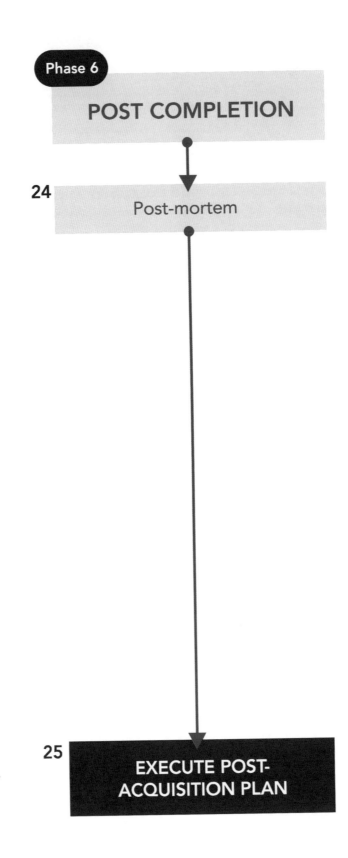

Phase 6

POST COMPLETION

24 Post-mortem

25 EXECUTE POST-ACQUISITION PLAN

- Culture is the corollary of a set of actions. You can't execute culture. You can continually hire and fire people, and that will create a certain culture. You can continually pay exorbitant bonuses, and that will create a certain culture. As a leadership team, you can act with professionalism, honesty, clarity, and that will also create a certain type of culture. Your choice.

Don't be naive about culture. In the context of acquisitions, it will be crucial to every type of integration plan. Diagnose each situation on its merits, and be prepared to walk away if the cultural fit looks weak.

Acquisitions can be a powerful tool to execute your strategy, but they are a graveyard of failures, missed opportunities, and under delivered promises. Why?

FINAL THOUGHTS - WHY ACQUISITIONS FAIL

Acquisitions can be a very effective way of driving growth. Acquisitions can be a powerful tool to execute your strategy, but they are a graveyard of failures, missed opportunities, and under delivered promises. Why?

I've studied the research, I've completed dozens of deals, I've failed to close many deals, and on that basis I offer my top reasons why you, too, may fail to close. Hope it helps.

TOP 10 REASONS

- Acquirers buy what's up for sale instead of what really fits their strategy. An acquisition profile is not created, and a formal search process is not conducted.
- The acquired company is not in the business the acquirer thought it was. A transport business buys an ambulance business. The latter is in the hospital sector, not the transport sector. The deal is a failure.
- The acquirer fails to learn from successive deals. No post mortems are conducted, and the same mistakes are repeated every time.
- There is no process map in place to execute acquisitions with the result that disparate teams, from finance to technical assessment experts, are not on the same page, and the project implodes.
- Post-acquisition planning is relegated to the last minute, either just prior to completion or just after completion. Result—integration is never truly achieved, key people leave, and the original ROI is never achieved.
- Commercial due diligence is done badly resulting in a flawed strategic case for the deal. The acquirer gets emotionally attached to closing the deal and ends up acquiring a business that was always a bad fit.
- The acquirer underestimates the talent being acquired, fails to integrate the key staff who made the target a success, and the acquired company declines, leading to a slow death. Most acquirers lose the selling company's management team in the first year.
- Preparation for the negotiation of price and deal structure is weak leading to overpriced and badly structured deals.
- Acquirers get confused between deferred consideration and earn-outs. The former are time-related payments with no performance requirements, and the latter are only paid by achievement of performances above historical results.
- Integration of targets is not driven by a senior director responsible for the success of the deal.

The Acquisition Approvals Model, if well-executed, will help avoid these pitfalls. This little book will change the way you buy companies. It will force your post-acquisition integration plan to the top of the agenda. It will significantly change the odds of successfully completing the right deals at the right price and integrating them seamlessly. Good luck!

HOW MUCH AM I WORTH?

How Much Am I Worth?

The Kelley Blue Book for second hand companies doesn't exist, but hopefully this appendix will explain how a buyer thinks when valuing acquisition targets.

Basically you need to establish some key facts and understand the basic formulas used, recognizing that each sector will have their favorite methods. Academics will tell you there are at least 6 ways of valuing businesses: the Price Earnings (PE) Ratio, Return on Investment (ROI), Multiple of Sales, Multiple of Gross Margin, Net Assets of the balance sheet, and Discounted Sustainable Cash Flows of the target.

In reality, most buyers of private companies will lean heavily on two, the PE Ratio and/or a Multiple of Sales. Once valued, the acquirer will compare the value with net assets being acquired, and the difference is technically and emotionally called goodwill. Forecasting cash generation 10 years out into the future and discounting those back to today is too unreliable for most acquirers. However, cash flow plays a big part in how VCs assess an investment opportunity.

So, the obvious questions to ask: what multiple? what PE to use? and what is the definition of profit?

WHAT PROFIT MULTIPLIER TO USE?

You need to gather some key PE ratios and then apply a little experience.
For illustrative purposes only, I'm using these data points from Dec 2013.

These ratios come from various sources: Lines 1 to 8 are extracted from Y Charts data on 4739 US public companies from a market worth of $435Bn to as small as $450,000! Find your specific sector by finding the Y Chart data table. The UK column is based on the FTSE Actuaries Share Indices table.

LINE		PE RATIOS			
		PUBLIC US	PUBLIC UK	PRIVATE US	PRIVATE UK
	Sector Averages (Dec 3 2013)				
1.	Staffing Services	31.39	23.62		
2.	Basic Materials	31.93	11.41		
3.	Industrials	16.96	23.82		
4.	Consumer Goods	12.47	16.48		
5.	Healthcare	21.20	19.88		
6.	Utilities	18.44	11.42		
7.	Financials	10.21	17.93		
8.	Technology	26.41	34.47		
	Key Summary Ratios				
9.	Average US private deals 2012 - Acquisions Monthly (assumption)			15.50	
10.	FTSE top 100 companies Nov 29		13.59		
11.	Leading Edge Alliance Tables - 2012 - PE derived from EBITDA Tables				10.00
12.	Robert Shiller S&P 500 PE 10	25.25			
13.	Long Term Average	15.50			

Remember, these are averages, and individual companies within these sectors could have wildly different PE ratios to these. Line 9 is an assumption for the purpose of this example, but more importantly, using Acquisitions Monthly or an equivalent database, it is possible to analyze deals completed in your sector, and some will disclose sufficient information to get a comparable PE ratio. Line 11 is an actual average from the Leading Edge Alliance tables from 2012, covering Europe. Line 10 is the average PE ratio for the top UK companies on that day. Line 12 is the Robert Shiller (Yale professor) PE index of the S&P 500 based on the average profits over the last 10 years, and he often compares that with the long term average PE, line 13. These are the types of ratios you need to assemble to come up with a fair multiple that an acquirer might apply to an established target company.

So, let's bring it together with an example. Let's say you are a recruitment business within the staffing services sector. The nearest competitor is On Assignment with a PE of 27.17, and the sector average for staffing services is 31.39. And, as a working assumption, let's say that deals completed in your sector are achieving a PE of 14. Also, let's assume you have a significant market share and all major factors (see final heading below) are normal. Given these facts, in my view, an acquirer will be assessing you at around a PE range of 14 to 18. The acquirer wants to avoid paying more than the sector averages of public companies and the acquirer's own PE.

What Profit to Use?

Most acquirers want to understand the sustainable level of post-tax profits from the target. The most common approach is to take the average of the previous 3 years audited profits pre-tax, add the current years forecast, and apply the acquirer's full year tax charge. The profits making up the average will be "normalized" by adjusting for exceptional items, such as: costs associated with a major factory relocation, large exceptional bad debt write offs, large unusual long term bonuses or unreasonably high base salaries, daughter's horse box expenses, Spanish sales office near the beach, adjustments required to be compliant with GAAP. Of course, any adjustment adding to profits will be debated vigorously by the acquirer!

Valuation Range

Therefore, assuming a sustainable post-tax profit of, say, $3m is produced from the calculations and applying the PE range of 14 to 18, we arrive at a valuation range of $42m to $54m. If the balance sheet showed net assets of $10m, you would be valuing goodwill at a minimum of $32m.

The Sales Multiplier

Of course, some sectors have a very specific way of calculating value, based on the future potential of owning the target. In software, the common basis is a multiple of sales. Over the last 24 months, the current valuation multipliers based on sales have risen dramatically. The graph below, from a recent blog post from venture capitalist Tomasz Tunguz, is both stunning and scary!

SaaS Enterprise Value to Revenue Trend Since 2004

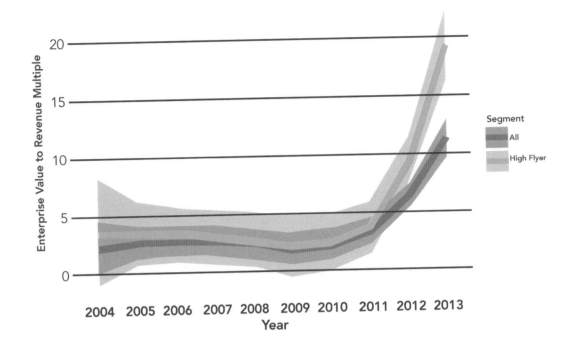

This is saying that some high-flying public companies are being valued at 20 times sales. Twitter and LinkedIn are valued even higher than that. The only rational explanation centers on the belief that these companies will produce ferocious growth in the short term, thus making the valuations look reasonable. However, you really are building a significant premium into today's price for tomorrow's results. Of course, if we bring the analysis up to date to, say, March 2015, we find a significant drop. As Tomasz points out in a recent post, "Over the last 15 months, the typical high growth public SaaS company's multiple has halved." His analysis shows that high growth companies peaked in February 2014 at about 22x forward revenues and have fallen to 11x by March 1, 2015.

FURTHER FACTORS

Factors to bear in mind that will seriously impact the perception of value by the acquirer include:

- Dependence on the owner
- Dependence on a few customers
- Historical growth rates
- Quality of product pipeline

- IPR or lack of it
- Competence of second tier management
- Market share
- Minimum size, attractive valuations are difficult to achieve when sales are less than $10m.
- Sales pipeline
- Simple share structure
- One year of losses will require at least 2 great years of profits immediately after those losses.
- Finally, the logic above clearly doesn't apply to loss-making start-ups acquired for their technology (and they are rare).

I hope that gives you some insights into the logic of valuation.

Overall, an acquirer perceives value and a seller aspires to price.

The great news is that once owners are armed with this knowledge, it is possible to action operational changes to increase the chances of cashing out at a premium price.

FURTHER HELP

Reach out to me at ian.smith@portfoliopartnership.com to discuss your Acquisition issues or call 978 395 1155

REFERENCES

Collins, Jim, and Morten Hansen. *Great by Choice*. HarperCollins: New York, 2011. Print.

Heimeriks, Koen H., Stephen Gates, and Maurizo Zollo. "The Secrets of Successful Acquisitions." *WSJ. Wall Street Journal*, 22 Sept. 2008. Web.

Moeller, Scott. "The Good, the Bad, and the Ugly: A Guide to M&As in Distressed Times." *cassknowledge*. CassBusinessSchool, 13 Jan. 2010. Web.

Tunguz, Thomasz. "The Forces in Tension in the SaaS Fundraising Market. Blog. *LinkedIn*. 18 March 2015. Web.

Tunguz, Tomasz. "The SaaS Valuation Bubble." Graph. [SaaS Enterprise Value to Revenue since 2204.] *tomasztungus.com*. N.p., 2013. Web.

Made in the USA
Lexington, KY
01 June 2017